# DINNER *by*
# *Candlelight*

# DINNER *by* Candlelight

## *Comfort and Joy for Advent*

KEVIN LOUISE SCHANER

XULON PRESS

Xulon Press
2301 Lucien Way #415
Maitland, FL 32751
407.339.4217
www.xulonpress.com

Unless otherwise indicated, Scripture quotations taken from New
Revised Standard Version (NRSV). Copyright © 1989 by Cokesbury

Printed in the United States of America.

ISBN-13: 978-1-54560-815-9

# DEDICATION

Thank you to my parents,
Henry and Celeste Hoop,
for gifting me with the Unconditional Love
that came down at Christmas.

# CONTENTS

# ACKNOWLEDGMENTS

To my writer-friends:

Sue Palmer and the Writers' Guild at Church of the Saviour United Methodist in Cleveland Heights, Ohio.

Betsy McMillan and the Water's Edge Writer's Meetup at the Kirkland Public Library in Kirkland, Ohio.

To my many first-draft readers who helped me to broaden my ideas into a book that is now more than my initial need to write it.

To my editor, Vickie Weaver of Writestyle, in West Carrollton, Ohio.

To my illustrator, Peg Weissbrod, in Cleveland, Ohio.

Any and all who have supported and aided me throughout this endeavor have my deep appreciation for their caring, ideas, suggestions and recommendations, expertise, and attention to detail.

# AN INVITATION TO
# THE READER

*A*dvent is the first season of the Christian year, and it arrives during the last month of our calendar year. I love the fact that the word Advent is from a Latin term that means "coming." I also think of anticipation, expectation, and renewal. Each of the four Sundays in Advent has a theme; we are invited to rediscover Hope, Love, Joy, and Peace and to light a candle for each theme during its week of our Advent journey. I view these themes as being old friends whom I need to keep close by; this is why I capitalize their names.

Does preparing for Christmas trigger a range of emotions for you? It does for me. Advent can be the most-challenging time of year. A lifetime of changes seem more obvious in December: adult children away from home, caring for elderly parents, or loss of relationships. Expected tasks and our longing for Christmases past can keep us from the full Joy of Christmas.

These essays are intended for comfort and Joy. I offer comfort in the Hope that we can accept change and suggestions to help us return to celebrating the birth of Jesus with Joy. I wrote this book because I was holding on to memories and traditions that were no longer possible while I needed to return to the Joy of His birth. Logically, I figured that others, too, have had some of these feelings. The people who were involved with the first Christmas had great faith, and we can still learn something from them; I have respectfully capitalized their names and titles, too. I encourage the acceptance of changes in our lives and inspire us to continue to find Joy in the season of Advent when our children are grown and we may be alone.

You can read these essays in any order either one a day or all at once. I invite you to consider the Christmas Conversation questions that you will find at the end of each essay. Talking about

Christmas may help us to move forward. In our world of high tech, we may be able to touch someone's life very easily during a time when discussion would be welcome. I encourage you to read and to discuss these essays with women in small groups at your church, with your co-workers at lunchtime, or while talking on your phone with family members. Even though we come from different places, we have common bonds at Christmas. Sharing our experiences builds relationships not only with each other but also with Christ. I invite you to extend your discussion with a broader audience at www.dinnerbycandlelight.blog. Or, you may feel more comfortable to have a private conversation with God. Also, suggested Advent Actions are included to encourage you to embrace change and to start new traditions. Please try only the ones that inspire you.

I hope that you will reread the essays and do more of the Advent Actions next year because you may relate to them in a different way.

Let's experience the rebirth of Christmas Joy as we journey back to Bethlehem and move forward with Christ in our lives throughout the year. Just as the three Wise Men went forth from Bethlehem in a different direction, let's find the way to spread the comforting news and the Joy of His birth.

# HOPE

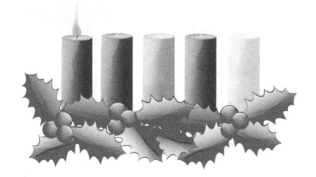

# DINNER BY CANDLELIGHT

*I*t was time to light the first candle, for Hope, on my Advent wreath. I did not light it last year, and I was not sure that I could light it this year. Longing for the comfort of Christmases past, I was afraid that finding the Joy associated with the birth of Jesus was not possible for me.

The days were growing shorter and darker. Because I now lived alone, I felt uncertain about observing Advent and rediscovering the Advent themes of Hope, Love, Joy, and Peace. Recently my life had been immersed in emotions related to situations where I was "going," the opposite of "coming." I was recently relocated, retired, and divorced. Despite the unexpected changes, I wanted to move forward, but I was afraid. According to the Gospel of Luke, even those involved in the first Christmas needed to be told not to be frightened when events were unfolding that would lead to the birth of Jesus; Zachariah, Mary, Joseph, and the awestruck Shepherds, surprised in their fields, were instructed by illumined Angels who reassured them, "Do not be afraid." Anxious to find out if I could bring light back into my life, I thought maybe I should start by counting the days to Christmas.

During the last year, I had determined that cooking for one was just not worthwhile and had chosen to eat my microwaved dinner in front of the television. It did not matter to me if I was dining with newscaster Brian Williams or playing "Jeopardy" with Alex Trebec; I just did not want to eat alone. Somehow I felt like I was having a conversation with them, even without dialogue. This was the first time in my life that the television was a comforting companion for me at mealtime. After Thanksgiving, I realized that I could break this habit if I could return to the tradition of lighting an Advent wreath during dinner; I decided to try.

On the first Sunday in Advent, I unpacked our family's ceramic Advent wreath and the memories of our years of lighting it. Because it

3

had been stored in my unheated attic, the brown circle was cold to my touch. Even the coolness felt familiar as my heart was warmed by the knowledge that the round shape symbolized God's never-ending love. Around the base, my fingers traced familiar faith symbols: Noah's ark, an anchor, and an open Bible. I concentrated on the Star of Bethlehem for my new direction.

The unopened package of Advent candles was still in the box from last year. Cellophane crinkled and clung to my fingers as I pulled the clear strips from the candles; three purple ones represented Hope, Love, Peace, and royalty for a King while a pink one was for Joy. I actually felt a little joyful. Was that a hint that former Christmas joys, even tiny ones, could resurface and comfort me? The holes in the wreath were clogged with wax that broke away when I twisted the candles into place. The wreath was ready for Advent. Was I? Could I discipline myself to have dinner with Jesus rather than commercial television?

I placed a white Christ candle in the middle of the wreath to light on Christmas Day. It seemed that in recent years the weeks of preparation for Christmas had zoomed by. Now, though, I dreaded the days of December. All of the candles are the same height today. If I follow the expected routine, the candles will be like a timely bar graph leading me to Christmas Day, and even if I am alone I may feel better about lighting the Christ candle.

I cautiously lit the Hope candle. My body sighed. Of the four Advent themes, Hope was the one that I needed to rekindle the most.

To my surprise, switching from watching television in the dim basement to lighting bright candles in my kitchen was easier than I had expected. I loved returning to the Advent wreath-lighting ritual. Even my Lean Cuisine meal tasted better by candlelight. Sitting at the table by myself with a candle glowing wasn't so bad. I did not miss the one-sided chatter from people on television; I appreciated the quiet while I read from an Advent devotional and was comforted by having a conversation with God. I felt good to return to something as simple and secure as sitting at a table to eat. A feeling that I was becoming more forward thinking came over me when I decided that cooking a batch of chili would be worthwhile. This meant that I could look forward to a home-cooked candlelight meal for several nights. Plus, at least during Advent, perhaps I should invite another person who is eating alone to my new home for chili and conversation.

Taking that first key step with Hope was putting me on a path out of fear toward true enjoyment of Advent again. I no longer felt alone because I was celebrating the coming of Jesus with my global Christian family. Until now, I had been anxious about dwelling on memories, both good and bad, and this had prevented me from being able to make new ones. I still had some longing for memories of Christmases past, but I was less fearful about Christmas coming. During quiet time each night, I was comforted to have my sadness gradually replaced with Joy. During the first week of Advent, I was grateful to God and proud of myself for overcoming the uneasiness I felt about how to celebrate Christmas differently. After contemplating the Hope candle for a week, I knew that I could look forward to lighting candles for Love, Joy, and Peace.

Advent is the season to expect Christmas coming, with Hope.

**Christmas Conversation:**

Think about the beginning of this Advent season.

This year, do you anticipate that preparing for Christmas will be hard for you or easy?

What rituals or disciplines do you observe during Advent? Do they truly bring you Hope, Love, Joy, and/or Peace? If so, how/why? Or, are there ones you wish to begin?

**Advent Action:**

Hope, Love, Joy, and Peace are themes for the four Advent Sundays. On which do you need to focus this year? If a certain one might bring even more comfort than the others, which will it be? Can you also help someone else to focus on one or more of these themes? If so, whom do you feel most compelled to help?

# TIMELESS TOWN

*B*ethlehem is a timeless town. As believers in Christ, we feel as if we have been there many times, even when we have not stepped a foot into the city. Our image of Bethlehem is most likely one that we have seen on a Christmas card: an ancient silhouette skyline illuminated by a star. Or, perhaps we visualize this holy city when we sing, "O, Little Town of Bethlehem."

Before the birth of Jesus, it was an insignificant little town located five miles south of Jerusalem. Joseph and Mary traveled to this City of David in order to be counted in the census decreed by Caesar Augustus. They passed through the arid hills into a walled city of houses built in front of caves. Perhaps Jesus was born in such a place.

In the Old Testament, Bethlehem was prophesied to be the place of the birth of the Messiah (Micah 5:2). Yet, until this time, it was unimportant in history, but now God is using it to call insignificant people. Bethlehem means "house of bread" and Jesus referred to himself as "the Bread of Life" (John 6:35).

Now, as we journey back to Bethlehem, we welcome the annual opportunity to get reacquainted with all those who were present when Jesus was born. Additional essays in this book will encourage you to look deeper into their roles and ask you to consider how you might relate to them. Many of us have known these Biblical characters since childhood. Each Advent, some of us are invited to rediscover their faith; as a result, we may learn more about our own.

During Advent, Bethlehem will move to the top of the list of places to be visited, if only in our hearts. We travel without the need of a reservation, but we may have some reservations. No need for a MapQuest search or a GPS; we know where we are headed. We can identify where, but we are not sure if our journey will be like Mary's swaying on a donkey or bumpy like each of the Magi on a camel.

In the Bible, four times in Luke's account involving the first Christmas, we read the phrase, "Do not be afraid." Angels cautioned Zechariah, Mary, Joseph, and the Shepherds. Just as they found comfort in his words, we should not be afraid to try new experiences. In recognition of the events of Jesus' birth, many still make a pilgrimage to Bethlehem. Nowadays, with continued conflict in the Middle East, travelers to Bethlehem are asked, "Aren't you afraid?" Fear can rule our hearts at any time.

An event that happened over two thousand years ago brought Hope and continues to change the world. One of my mom's favorite quotes was Dr. Ralph W. Sockman's: "The hinge of history is on the door of a Bethlehem stable."

## Christmas Conversations:

Think about the significance of Bethlehem as a timeless town.

Why do you think Jesus was born in a humble, insignificant place?

Of the characters in the Christmas story, who do you think were initially the most afraid?

The last line of "O, Little Town of Bethlehem" says: "O come to us, abide with us, our Lord Emmanuel." What does this mean to you? Does it make you feel hopeful?

## Advent Actions:

Make a list of the names of groups or people whom you associate with the town of Bethlehem. Who were viewed as being insignificant? Who were viewed as being important at the time?

Although you may feel insignificant at times, what are the ways that you show God's love by your service?

# ADVENT CALENDARS

Two years ago, I rescued an Advent calendar from our church's flea market. Twenty-five golden felt rectangles of various sizes framed the people, animals, and objects related to the birth of Jesus. I wish that you could see the intricate blanket-stitches that outline each and the sequins, cording, and seed beads that make it a work of art. What was this doing at a flea market? Someone had lovingly created it. Why wasn't it kept as a family keepsake? My heart ached that there was no one to treasure it, so I brought it home. I felt an emotional attachment to this felt wall-hanging because it reminded me of my previous "countdown to Christmas" experiences and of the Advent calendars I had created for my family.

My first Advent calendar was a paper chain, twenty-four strips of construction paper stapled together. The loops hung on a single nail for this purpose on the back of our front door. I was only seven years old, but I still remember that each day in December I tore off a paper link. I could not wait to do this each morning before I walked to school. The excitement of a lone link meant that Santa would come that night.

At the time, I did not know this was an Advent calendar. For me, it was more of a countdown to Christmas. Later my Baltimore aunt sent me a more-traditional calendar. It had numbered windows to open each day, with tabs on an elaborate Nativity scene. My fingers got glittery as I opened each. On December 24th I found Baby Jesus in the manger.

German Protestants during the nineteenth century were the first to mark the days of Advent. They drew chalk lines on their doors and lit candles to count the days leading to Christmas. Advent calendars were available in different styles. I unexpectedly received one when I was a young mom. "Open on Arrival" were the handwritten directions on an early box from my sister-in-law in Colorado. I was surprised to find an Advent calendar. Just as when I was a child, I could not wait to open the compartments that decorated the photograph of a large snow-covered evergreen. Inside were miniature wooden ornaments of a doll, a drum, and a wagon that were my favorites, until I found Baby Jesus.

During the 1980s, counted cross-stitch embroidery was popular. Patterns for ornaments that could be framed inside a one-inch brass ring were the ones I preferred to stitch. I used these to create an Advent calendar. The designs included Angels, packages, wreaths, ornaments, Shepherds, and a manger. Because I needed twenty-four, I selected different-colored embroidery floss for many of the patterns so that each would be unique. Of course, there was one Baby Jesus. Red Velcro dots trimmed the green felt tree that waited for an ornament to be attached each day.

You can never be too old for an Advent calendar to inspire anticipation and Hope. I enjoyed the childlike feeling of the Christmas countdown so much that I duplicated this project and made a calendar for Henry's Upholstering, my dad's shop. A Christmas tree was always placed in the storefront window, so it was easy to view the green felt calendar that hung beside it.

One Advent calendar that I had created and filled before our sons were born became a part of our family celebration. Each morning Owen and Neil took turns and placed an ornament on the tree. They did this faithfully every December, even when they were in high school. After Owen left for college, Neil decorated it by himself. A year later, my heart was heavy when the Advent-calendar tradition returned to being mine alone.

Preparations for Christmas will change. Each year as I place the final ornament with Baby Jesus on the tree, I am reminded that He is the same.

## Christmas Conversations:

Think about ways you have counted down to Christmas.

Do you need or want a new way to count down?

Describe an Advent calendar that was in your life.

Do you think that having a countdown of some kind helps us to focus more on the birth of Jesus? To feel hopeful? If so, why/how?

## Advent Actions:

Introduce the Advent calendar tradition to someone of any age. Tell that person the ways you have counted down to Christmas.

# Hope Reborn

One year Advent saved my life.

An unexpected tragedy came into our lives before the start of the season of expectation. On Thanksgiving Day, just three days before it was time to start lighting the Advent wreath, our first baby, a daughter, was stillborn. No specific cause was found; she was full term. I still remember the deafening silence of the delivery room.

We were numb when we left the hospital. This unexpected outcome left us feeling empty at a time when we had expected our lives to be even more full than usual. We returned to an apartment that had a room ready for a baby, but without a baby for the crib. Sad, sad, sad is how we felt. The memorial service on Saturday brought our families together. Because we had expected December to be filled with the demands of an infant and the uncertainties of learning how to be parents, we had completed our gift buying before Thanksgiving; we sent the wrapped Christmas presents home with family members following the service. With our expectations for this time unfulfilled, we wondered: What will we do now?

It may be hard to believe, but we managed to attend the evening service at church on that first Sunday in Advent. We welcomed hugs from our church family, who needed reassurance from us. During this time when we received comfort, we were often the comforters. Some friends did not know what to say to us, and others were as upset as if they had lost their own baby. We were not expecting to need to console our friends, but we did so. Watching the lighting of the Advent candle gave us a small flicker of hope that with Christmas coming, we could start to move forward.

Surviving the first week without our baby was hard. Because I was on maternity leave and my husband was looking for employment, we used this time to grieve together. We cried so much that our pillows were ruined and we had to throw them away; our next outing was to buy new ones. The outside world saw a young woman Christmas shopping, but inside I wanted to shout to them, "I just lost my baby!" Our personal world of friends let us know in many ways that they were thinking about us. We wrote thank-you notes for the poinsettias and meals that were brought. I recall preparing our Christmas cards, adding an unexpected-outcome note for those who needed it. My physical pain when my milk came in could be matched only by my emotional distress. Receiving mail each day was both sorrowful and comforting; we were sad because the cards were not pink baby ones, but consoled because obviously so many people cared about us. We read one hundred sympathy cards.

Our December days were slow, silent, and blurred by tears. But, we trimmed a tree. We marked our days of grief and gradual recovery while lighting our Advent wreath at home and reading from a daily devotional. We tried to relate to Peace, Love, Hope, and Joy. Peace of mind that it was not our fault that we were not holding our own baby; love from others; but mostly hope that we would feel joy, again.

Our original plan was to celebrate Christmas in our apartment, our home, once we had children. Instead, we placed all the baby items into a storage locker and drove to southern Ohio to be with our families. Because I could not bear to take them down, the curtains with the toy theme remained in the spare bedroom with our hopes.

When Christmas Eve arrived, we were relieved. We had survived a month of living, grieving, and healing. Attending the service in the church where I grew up was comforting in a way that I had not expected. When candlelight filled the sanctuary it was as if it were a new day; I was grateful for how Advent had given me a faithful focus. Our Hope was reborn because we could center our lives on the birth of Jesus. But, the memory of the silent delivery room still haunted me. Perhaps after another year I would be able to join in the singing of "Silent Night."

Because Jesus was born, our Hope was reborn.

**Christmas Conversations:**

Think about a time in your life or the life of someone you know when you or that person needed Hope to survive. What helped you or that person to cope? Is that memory with you during every Advent? Why do you think that memory returns each year?

What is your definition for Hope?

How are healing and Hope related in our Christian lives?

**Advent Action:**

Reflect on this verse, as stated in *The Message.* "The mere sound of His name will signal hope" (Matthew 12:21).

# CALLED BY NAME

*H*ow could a little baby have so many names? Bambino, Emmanuel, Gesu, and Saviour are names we affectionately sing during the Advent season as we anticipate His birth.

"Little Sweetie" is what I lovingly whispered to second son Neil as I welcomed him into the world. What about Mary? Did she exclaim an endearing term heard only by father Joseph and treasured? A name not to be recorded outside the humble stable.

Or, did she call Him Jesus from the first moment? Of all the stresses Mary must have had, naming her baby was not one of them. It is recorded in the first chapter of Matthew, verse 21, that the Angel Gabriel said to her, "You will bear a son, and you are to name him Jesus..." It turns out that Jesus was a common name in first-century Galilee. I wonder if Mary wished the predetermined name could be more unique. Or, maybe she was relieved, compared with the shocking news of being pregnant, that she was glad He would have a name that would not make Him stand out.

Nowadays, no amount of effort is considered too much when it comes to selecting the name for our offspring. We consider family names, popular ones and one of a kind, as we pore over baby-naming books and Web sites. We consider name origins and what they mean. Some undecided families in the delivery room would no doubt welcome the chance to hear the name of their babies announced by an angel.

We were ready with a name when our first son was baptized during Advent. "What name shall be given this child?" the minister asked. Owen Patrick Schaner was dressed in the flowing white gown that his paternal grandfather had worn for his ceremony. During this special moment, we were concentrating on the name we gave to Owen, not on the future names that would describe his roles in life.

When Jesus was born as a Saviour, He already had names other than Jesus. Scholars divide the Bible's over two hundred names for Jesus into three categories. Holy One, Judge, and Word or Word of Life are examples for the nature of Christ. Alpha and Omega, Lord of All, and True God are assigned to His position in the tri-unity of God group. Finally, His work on Earth includes names such as Bridegroom, Rock, and True Vine.

We may have many names throughout our lives, but we will not have as many as Jesus. Rather than concentrating on our personal given names, it is more important for us to recognize that each of us is a child of God because "He knows everyone's name" (Psalms 91:14).

During Advent, we begin this sacred season with the endearing names for the Christ Child. By the end of the month we are comfortable to call Him by many more. Can you hear His names during Handel's *Messiah*? "Wonderful, Counselor, Mighty God, the Everlasting Father, the Prince of Peace..." Each of them makes me feel Hope in my heart.

### Christmas Conversations:

Consider your thought process of naming a baby or someone you know who did.

Were you concerned that it would be a popular name? That it would or would not stand out? If so, what were your concerns and what were your reasons for each?

What are the different names that you are called? Which ones do you cherish?

Reconsider the theme of Hope. Which name for Jesus makes you feel hopeful? Does one name for Jesus say Hope? Which one?

### Advent Actions:

Make a list of names for Jesus. Some could already be known to you; others may come newly from your heart. Which one or ones do you lean toward?

# LEAP FOR JOY

*M*ary had a miraculous secret. Was it really possible that the Angel Gabriel had told her that she soon would be with child? And that she had said, "Okay"? Who would believe this?

As we prepare for Advent, we anticipate sharing spiritual joys with our friends and families. What could top the Holy Spirit's bonding story of Elizabeth and Mary? Elizabeth, Mary's relative, was old enough to be Mary's mother. She and her husband were right with God but childless. Gabriel told them that their prayer had been heard—they could expect a son.

Mary learned after her own shock that Elizabeth, too, was expecting. Perhaps she was comforted to hear of another conception miracle. There had not been such a miracle in over four hundred years. But now, two women who should not be pregnant were going to have babies and she was one of them. Mary expected Elizabeth to accept her.

It was unusual for a woman to travel alone at that time. Yet, young Mary journeyed over eighty miles into the hill country to the city of Judah. She had three more days to ponder her situation, which no human except Elizabeth could comprehend. Did Mary feel excited, embarrassed, or afraid? Did she pray to understand that all things are possible with God?

Today, for confirmation of pregnancy we likely would use a drugstore test kit or visit a doctor. Or, we might mention to our moms, "I feel really tired and my breasts are sore," and the mom may comment that she had felt that way when she was pregnant. In contrast, Mary was not expecting to hear that she was expecting. At least she was told, "Do not be afraid."

I have always loved this visitation story because I could relate to Mary's excitement to share her secret. Elizabeth could not hide hers; she was six months along. Gabriel had revealed to Zechariah, the baby's father, that their son would be called John. This couple's proof that all things are possible with God would reassure Mary in her own faith. During traditional greetings there would have been hours of conversation. Don't we wish that we could have overheard this one?

When the miracle moms met, Elizabeth exclaimed that her baby, John, had a "Leap for Joy" at the sight of Mary and that she herself was filled with the Holy Spirit. Mary responded with her song that glorified the Lord. A painting by Brigid Marlin depicting this visitation expresses their age difference through symbolism: Elizabeth stands by a mature fruit tree and Mary in front of a blossoming younger tree, both in traditional dress. We see inside their wombs; the identity of Christ is recognized by John's leap and by Elizabeth when she feels it.

It was nearly time for Elizabeth to deliver when Mary returned home three months later. She had witnessed the growth of her kinswoman's swollen belly and was comforted. Mary had leapt for Joy at what God could do because everything is possible with God.

**Christmas Conversation:**

Think about an event that you could not wait to share in your life or someone you know who had such an experience.

To whom do you turn to share your Hope, Joys, and concerns?

Whom do you pray with?

**Advent Actions:**

Look on the Internet for Brigid Marlin's painting titled, *"The Visitation of Elizabeth by Mary."*

Think about the Hope in John's "Leap for Joy" as you read Mary's Song in Luke 1:46–55.

# African Crèche

*M*y friend Gwen loves babies. She has cuddled ones named Blessing, Comfort, and Patience. Twice we journeyed together on Volunteer In Mission teams to Zimbabwe, Africa. My fondest memory of those trips is the contentment on her face as she snuggled a boy named Valentine. I wonder who was comforted more as his hand gently caressed her cheeks.

The first time that we visited, Gwen and I were overwhelmed by conditions at Fairfield Children's Home at Old Mutare Mission. Children stampeded to greet us and tackled our knees until we fell to the ground. Fifty children and two adult caregivers were in one large room of chaos. Each child was desperate for a loving touch and individual attention. With no electricity, meeting the daily physical needs of so many children was a challenge. Some teenagers on our team played with preschoolers at the overused playground while others cradled infants at the baby-fold near the hospital. Helpless would be a good word to describe how we felt.

Back in Ohio we projected pictures of sudza (porridge) bubbling over a smoky fire. We sighed at the images of the children clinging to our clothes as we stood by miles of clothesline containing their hand-washed miniature shirts, shorts, and underpants. Needing a plan to help us improve their lives and their caregivers', we decided that our annual Cookie Walk during Advent would be a fundraiser for them. Cranberry bars, chocolate mint drops, and glazed ginger snaps were some of the goodies that were lovingly produced to sell by the pound. We were grateful to the additional bakers and buyers at our church who have supported our Cookie Walk for sixteen years. Annually we have donated $1,000 toward the staff at Fairfield. We always sell more cookies in a few hours than "our children" in Zimbabwe will ever see.

Six years after our initial visit, Gwen and I returned to Fairfield Children's Home. The one-room facility had been replaced by individual houses. Gwen and I could not control our happy tears; we felt humbled to play a small part in a significant transformation and relieved that our Hopes had been realized. Each home had a family unit with an age range of children under the care of two women whom they called "Mom" and "Auntie." Children gently tugged our hands and led us toward their garden. "See our sweet potatoes?" they asked proudly. Others guided us to the small kitchen to meet the cooks who were chopping the vegetables for soup. In one house, we walked through the living room into the bedrooms. A child explained, "This is my bunkbed" as he patted the homemade comforter. Instead of grabbing us, kids were hugging each other now that they lived in a calmer, caring, and comforting environment.

Gwen got her baby fix when we visited the new preschool building called The Crèche. Traditionally, most of us think of a crèche as a model representing the scene of the birth of Jesus. Another definition for this term is nursery school. What a perfect name for a fun and safe space for orphans year round! During Advent, my concept of crèche has been rooted in the birthplace of Baby Jesus and is now extended to a blessed brick building in Africa where many will learn about Him.

**Christmas Conversations:**

Think about children and their needs at Christmas. What stands out the most to you?

How does your church or other organizations meet the needs of children for Christmas?

If you have been on a mission trip, what action project did you initiate or follow through on when you returned? How were you able to include those who were not on the trip? How did you feel about it?

**Advent Actions:**

Select and assist children in a different country through your prayers, service, or gifts.

For instance, HOLD a Cookie Walk as a fundraiser. BAKE homemade cookies. BRING them to tables and label the goodies. Containers, plastic gloves, and a commercial scale are all you need. PROMOTE your Cookie Walk so that people will select a variety of homemade cookies. WEIGH them at your checkout where customers BUY them by the pound. We charged $8 per pound. GIVE the money to your chosen group.

# LOVE

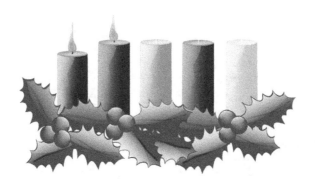

# POINSETTIA DELIVERY

The second week of Advent arrived—time for me to light another candle. The purple Love candle reminded me of the comforting support of my friends and church family and of our Advent expectation to receive and give love. Families may change, but God's love is constant.

Soon, December's poinsettia delivery was scheduled. That day at school I had told the Mexican legend about this flower to the children during their library class. I knew that Betty, my fellow church member, would also enjoy it when I visited her later; she was in nursing care at a facility during the years that I visited her monthly on my way home from work.

Betty looked perfect in a powder-blue pantsuit with her hair permed and styled and soft pink lipstick framing her smile. She was dozing as I pulled back the curtain that divided the room. A single hospital bed and an upholstered chair filled with stuffed animals and a knitted prayer shawl filled half of her space. My gentle touch on her shoulder brought a smile. She pointed to the pictures atop the dresser near the foot of her bed: her out-of-town daughters and her deceased husband of fifty years, Bob. A wheelchair and a walker crowded the floor, so I sat on the edge of the bed. As she patted my leg, I asked, "Do you remember decorating your tree? Being Santa for your girls? Attending the candlelight service at church?" Betty nodded and grinned as if a video of Christmas memories were streaming through her mind. She had a difficult time speaking; she communicated chiefly with her eyes and by waving her hands that flashed with her favorite red nail polish. When I placed the foil-wrapped potted poinsettia on her moveable tray table, she felt the velvety leaves and expressed appreciation with her smiling eyes. She listened with interest as I retold the story of a poor Mexican girl:

"Rosita was distressed because she had no gift to place at the manger during the Christmas Eve pageant. Her brother, Pepito, reminded her, 'Even the most humble gift, if given in love, will be acceptable in His eyes.' Rosita swallowed her pride and snatched some weeds as she entered the church. She tentatively bowed and offered her gift to Jesus. Suddenly, the green leaves were transformed into red star-like blooms both inside the sanctuary and outside. This is why the poinsettia is known as the Flower of the Holy Night."

Betty received nourishment from a feeding tube, so we shared Communion without actually partaking of the wafer and the grape juice. While saying the Lord's Prayer, "Our Father...," we were comforted by our ritual of the Upper Room. Knowing that her church family had sent the red poinsettia reminded her that we loved her and missed her. She pulled my arm to draw me closer to her lips and labored to explain: "In a dream I saw my father. I just want to go home and be with my father." I kissed her forehead; she squeezed my hand.

Like Rosita, we sometimes question what we have to offer. No doubt Betty felt this way about her present life when comparing it with her more-vibrant earlier one. I was humbled by her desire to share her most-intimate thoughts. In the loving gift of friendship, we shared the same Father.

**Christmas Conversations:**

Think about those who are either homebound or in a care facility.

How can you reach out to those who are isolated all year?

How do you think people feel about past celebrations in which they can no longer partake?

Share a situation where this verse applied to your life: "For where two or three are gathered in my name, I am among them" (Matthew 18:20).

Where are you expecting to find and communicate Love during this Advent?

**Advent Actions:**

Take a poinsettia to someone who is lonely and listen to his/her Christmas memories.

# THE GIFT OF RECEIVING

*M*y church participates in a project called Christmas Angels during Advent. Local agencies such as the Hunger Center and Prison Ministries supply the names of children who need to be remembered with a gift at Christmas. Members select a card with the child's name, clothing sizes, and a specific gift wish. Over the years I've had fun shopping for a pink watch, a Connect Four game, and even underwear. With the names of "our" children placed on the purchases, we return the unwrapped gifts to the church for delivery. On Christmas morning, I always think about "my" child and pray that her day was memorable.

It is easier to be a Christmas Angel to someone whom you do not know, compared with such an experience for people you do know. I am fortunate to have learned this from personal experience both as a child and as an adult.

When I was past the years of believing in Santa, my mom told me that she was grateful for local elves. My dad worked two jobs and provided for what we needed and for most of our wants. One year, a toy metal toaster was on my list and not likely to be delivered by Santa. The two-income family across the street volunteered to purchase something from my list. Click, click, click was the sound of the pink toaster as I pretended to prepare breakfast. My mom heard me say, "Thank you, thank you, thank you."

A transistor radio was the top gift requested by me and my fifth-grade friends as we started to venture into a world beyond toys. Mr. and Mrs. Vance, fellow church members, did not have children of their own, and they offered to buy the radio to be given to me by my parents. It must have been both a relief and a joy for my parents to see me unwrap the silver radio and place it into its brown leather case. Mom commented for years that it was the Christmas when I spent all of my vacation escaping into the musical world with plugs in my ears. I am glad that my parents shared with me about special friends who were givers and showed me how to be a gracious recipient. This taught me that it was okay to be like them, to be a receiver once in a while.

Years later when I was preparing for Christmas with our young family, my good friend and coworker gave me a special gift. "Open this when you get home. Merry Christmas!" she said as she hugged me. When I unsealed the card at home, I was surprised to find a fifty-dollar bill. Of course, I was grateful, and I also admired her courage to know and to fulfill a holiday need for my family. With her gift, I purchased the ingredients for Cornish hens and other goodies for our annual celebration with Owen and Neil's godparents.

My experiences of receiving from Christmas Angels as a child and as an adult taught me the importance of developing relationships and gaining courage to be a Christmas Angel for others. It takes guts to do it the first time, but the lasting memories of Love and generosity between the giver and the receiver are worthwhile.

**Christmas Conversations:**

Think about times in your life when you have been the "giver" and the "receiver."

What Christmas projects have you been involved with during Christmas for people whom you do not know? How does this make you feel?

Would you feel comfortable offering an unexpected gift to someone you know?

**Advent Actions:**

Consider how you could be a Christmas Angel to someone or a familiar family: with a gift, your time, or your prayers. If you can follow through, do so to help in bringing Hope, Love, Joy, and Peace.

# COME, EMMANUEL

When you hear the organist practicing, "O Come, O Come, Emmanuel," you know Advent is coming. Christmas music, possibly more than anything else, puts us in the mood for the season. We relate to songs in different ways according to our experiences, and we may feel different levels of expectation and Love.

When I attended elementary school, two popular carols were played on the radio that we also sang in church. I learned "The Little Drummer Boy" because I could sing along while playing my 45-rpm record. The record's jacket cover pictured a shepherd boy with his drum; I believed that he played for Jesus. Can you hear the "ding" of those tiny cymbals while you hum the "rum pum pum" chorus? The same composer wrote "Do You Hear What I Hear?" This was a trendy song for my sixth-grade chorus to learn. I practiced the descant part loudly in the kitchen while washing dishes each night. My focus was to perform well at the holiday concert. This song was written during the Cuban Missile Crisis in 1963 to "Pray for peace, people everywhere." As timely today as it was then.

The verses of a hymn tell a story, and I have a story about one of my favorites. The first Christmas CD that I put into the player begins with mumbling whispers and unclear voices. The muted sound makes me strain to hear whether these are specific words. The distant voices unexpectedly resonate closer and shout, "Go Tell It on the Mountain." Every time I hear the start to this hymn, the music takes me back to mornings at Old Mutare Mission in Zimbabwe. The unclear murmurs on this recording are just like the gentle whispers that drifted down at dawn from Mount Chirimba as the villagers started their day so peacefully. This "over the hill and everywhere" spiritual reminds me of when I felt the presence of the Holy Spirit while worshipping with the Shona people.

Back home, our choir processed into the sanctuary singing "On This Day Earth Shall Ring" for our service of lessons and carols. One year as a choir member, I marched down the center aisle and paused while we sang the chorus, "Id-e-o-o-o, id-e-o-o-o, ide-o Gloria in excelsis Deo!" The cadence of this hymn creates a feeling of community for me; it gives me goosebumps. I have a similar reaction when I hear the English carol "Tomorrow Shall Be My Dancing Day"; I love how the writer has Jesus tell his life story in His own voice, characterized as a dance.

Contemporary musicians continue to explore modern interpretations about Jesus as a baby boy. The song "Mary, Did You Know?" asks her questions to which we already know the answers. Had she thought about Him walking on water, saving sons and daughters, or ruling nations? When we see a young mother cradling her baby and representing Mary holding Jesus, the last line is real to us: "The sleeping child you're holding is the Great, I am."

One carol that I have experienced in different ways is "Oh, Holy Night." My mom thought no one could sing like the tenor Mario Lanza. After Thanksgiving, his was one of the first albums to spin on the hi-fi's turntable. The opportunity to hear the richness of his voice in our home was more than Mom could have imagined after she had lived in the deprivation of the Great Depression. More recently I have heard the words for this carol sung by a soprano, not a tenor. I appreciate that our music director selects a teenaged girl to sing "Oh, Holy Night." Her sweet soprano voice fills the sanctuary; we feel as if Mary is telling us, "This is the night of our dear Saviour's birth."

Then the sanctuary darkens, except for the Christ candle. The young girls dressed as angels each light a candle and take their positions in the aisles. We start to sing the beloved "Silent Night." The carol originally played on a guitar in Austria is now embellished with instruments throughout the world. With anticipation and awe, we wait as each candle is touched by a flame and the light spreads down each pew and across the aisles. On the last verse, we lift our candles in unison as we sing "Christ the Saviour is born." A deep sense of Love seems to envelope every believer there. Advent concludes with comfort and Joy to our Emmanuel.

**Christmas Conversations:**

Think about the music that you love for Advent. How does it make you feel?

Have your favorite carols or hymns changed? What experiences caused you to relate to them differently?

Which words in which song or songs move you toward preparing for the Love of Christ?

Which song(s) do you find yourself humming now and then during the remainder of the year?

Do you follow the tradition of lifting candles on a verse of "Silent Night"? Or, do you have another tradition with a carol?

**Advent Actions:**

Invite a friend or relative to attend a church service or a Christmas concert with you.

Go to the church of a friend or relative and experience how Christmas music is presented there. Compare how it made you feel with how your favorite hymns make you feel. Differences? Similarities?

# "SEEING" SANTA AND BABY JESUS

"*M*om, I saw him. I know I saw him!" I begged Mom to believe me. I *did* see Santa Claus with his reindeer flying across a starry midnight sky!

"You had better get to bed. You know that Santa only visits houses where the children are asleep," Mom frantically reminded me as I took a sip of water. No wonder parents had this commonly shared rule. At that moment, my parents were trying to be Mr. and Mrs. Claus in our living room. They believed in the total-love package of Christmas, which meant not only to set out the gifts but also to decorate the tree, to hang the stockings, and finally to eat the cookies that I had left for Santa.

The contents of a dusty carton stored eleven months of the year in our attic held the images of how I recall the loving miracles of Christmas Eve. Recently, I opened this box. As I unfolded the cardboard flaps, I saw the picture books and jigsaw puzzle that had helped me to "see" the unseen.

My few childhood books from the 1950s were mostly the Golden Book variety. I still treasure them because I remember when Mom read them to me. One of my December favorites was *Christmas Puppy.* What little girl would not be thrilled with a story about a black Cocker Spaniel puppy found inside a stocking on Christmas morning? I enjoyed this book as a kindergartener, and as a school librarian I shared it with the same age group.

When I was four years old, traditional illustrations in *T'was the Night before Christmas* convinced me that I did see Santa's sleigh in the sky. That book awakened my imagination while I tried to fall asleep on what seemed like the longest night of my life. Later, in the post Santa years, I was old enough to read Moore's classic by myself.

As I did, I was surprised to realize that the image of Santa on the cover was exactly what I had seen that night when I begged Mom to believe me. At the same time that I fantasized about Santa at the North Pole, I also learned about Jesus in Bethlehem.

In the Christmas box, under the Santa stories, I discovered the real meaning of Christmas. A large cardboard puzzle filled the bottom. With the pieces still in place, the puzzle presented a close-up view illuminated by a shining star inside the wooden-framed stable. Smiling Mary, sleeping Jesus, standing Joseph, kneeling Shepherds, and settling sheep had made me feel like I was with them on the night Jesus was born. The title of the puzzle announced "*Unto You a Child Is Born.*"

When I was Mrs. Claus for my own children, I hoped that Christmas would be as memorable for them as the night was for me when I truly saw Santa. Sixty years later, when I attend the tableau (Holy Family) service in the sanctuary of my church, I still visualize that first Christmas like the scene in my childhood puzzle.

**Christmas Conversations:**

Think about how you pictured Santa Claus or the setting for where Jesus was born.

When did you discover the truth about Santa? How did that truth help you to make a shift to focus on Jesus?

Recall a book, or painting, or medium that helped you to formulate what was in your mind. What about it helped you? Does it still make the connection for you?

Did "seeing" the unseen Jesus or manger scene help you to believe in the Holy Night? Do we have to see in order to believe?

Think of Christmas books you had as a child or that you shared with other children.

How do you think our media world will affect how children "see," experience, and remember the events of Christmas Eve?

**Advent Action:**

Read, share, or give one of your favorite Christmas books.

# BACKWARD SHEEP

*I*n the Christmas story, I felt that the characters to whom I could most relate were the Shepherds. When I was an elementary-school librarian, I thought of myself as "shepherding" or at least "herding" children in a gentle direction. This may also be why one of my favorite images of Jesus is as the Good Shepherd. Like Him, I went out of my way to rescue some students who were lost in regular school activities but found the library to be comfortable.

Finding the Shepherds and the sheep in the Nativity box was a memory I treasured from childhood. "Mom," I asked, "Why is this one sheep always looking backward?" I held up the big gawky one that looked like he had a "crook" in his neck. He looked out of place, compared with the smaller sheep in the set; like he belonged in a different Nativity. Each time we arranged the figures under the tree, we placed the Shepherds to the left of the Holy Family and the Wise Men to their right. Backward Sheep looked like he was searching. I decided to put him to the left of the Holy Family so that he appeared to look back to see if the Shepherds were getting closer to Jesus.

After I retired from my library career, difficult and unexpected changes happened in my life. Perhaps the familiarity of the figures in my childhood Nativity would bring me comfort during Advent, and I expected my experiences about how I viewed them to be the same. Backward Sheep was the first one I unwrapped, and I remembered that I considered him to be out of place. To my surprise, I felt very much like him.

Like Backward Sheep, my neck was bent out of shape. The traditions from past Christmases were no longer possible. I had moved to a different house with only an artificial tree, and I would not see my sons on Christmas Day. Nothing seemed normal. Even though I felt sad, I did not want to be comforted. My mood was in a dark place, and I did not know how to keep myself from feeling that way. I was not only a

Backward Sheep; I was also a lost one. Would future Christmases feel as lonely as this one? Would I ever feel my former Christmastime love and happiness again?

When I was a child, I had found a way to be satisfied with how Backward Sheep eventually fit into the Nativity. How could I find a way now to deal with my hopeless feelings and fit into this Advent? Instead of looking to the past, I needed to move forward. I decided to put Backward Sheep on the right side of Mary and Joseph; now, he was looking at Baby Jesus.

Changing his position helped me to change mine. I no longer felt like a lost sheep. When I had related to the Shepherds, I remembered how good I had felt when supporting students who needed comfort. Now, I could accept that I was the one searching for comfort. I remembered, "I am the Good Shepherd. I know my sheep and my sheep know me" (John 10:14, NIV). With my faith refocused on the Christ Child, I was ready to be found by the Good Shepherd and to feel Christmas comfort again.

**Christmas Conversations:**

Currently, how do you feel: more like a Shepherd or more like a sheep?

Can you think of a time when you or someone you know felt like a lost sheep? If you felt that way, write a verification of when you were one. Did someone help you? Or, did you find your own way? Did the memory warm your heart, make you laugh, or make you remember friends and loved ones as Backward Sheep? How does that make you feel now?

If you are feeling like a Backward Sheep right now, how could your relationship with Jesus help you to move forward?

**Advent Action:**

Reach out to someone who you know may be feeling like a "Backward Sheep" during this Advent.

# JEWELS IN A TREASURE BOX

"Walk home quickly. The first batch will be bubbling on the stove," Mom reminded me as I slipped out the back door to walk to school.

While attending elementary school, we had an hour and a half break in the middle of the day. I walked home every day for lunch. Soon after Thanksgiving, for about two and a half weeks, Mom and I used this time at noon to make hard candy together.

It was magical to me how white sugar and Karo syrup heated in a heavy metal pot could become hard candy. We watched the candy thermometer's red line creep to three hundred degrees. When it reached the hard-crack stage, Mom worked her magic. A wooden spoon was her wand when she stirred the red food coloring into the clear mixture. Our first batch was always flavored with cinnamon oil; that scent filled our kitchen. Now, it was time for us to work quickly before the concoction could set.

A sixteen-inch rimmed circular griddle was oiled and ready on the kitchen table. Mom gingerly carried the scalding pot from the stove. She needed both hands to tilt the handle and pour the liquid sugar. The molten mixture spread to the edge of the pan like lava.

"It looks like a stained glass window," I said, watching the procedure.

Mom used a spatula to test the edges to see if the candy was pliable. Was it ready to be cut into bite-sized pieces? Soon, she started to cut half-inch strips of candy and laid them on an oiled cookie sheet. "Start cutting as soon as you can touch them. Be careful," she cautioned.

I can still feel the ouchy burn as my fingers tried to touch the molten candy. Soon I used cooking shears to cut uniform diagonal pieces. Clank, clank, clank was the welcome sound as the triangles that resembled the jeweled points in a crown dropped onto the sheet.

It had been a year since we had savored cinnamon hard candy, and we were tempted to taste a piece before it cooled. Even today, no matter when I crunch into cinnamon hard candy, it tastes like Christmas.

We started with the Christmas colors, red and green. Cinnamon and wintergreen were our favorite flavors. These were followed by blue clove and white peppermint. Orange and lemon-yellow were the hardest batches to complete because the citric acid that was needed to complement these flavors caused the sugar to harden more quickly; we often were not able to create bite-sized pieces fast enough. When the final saucer-sized piece was too hard for the scissors to cut, we cracked it with a metal ice-cream scoop and it shattered. We had to accept that the delicious lemon and orange pieces were not perfect triangles.

Each new batch of hard candy was added to the multicolored mixture in the turkey-roasting pan. The candy clanked against the metal as we stirred with a wooden spoon. The colors were vibrant.

"They look like jewels in a treasure box," Mom said.

Yes, rubies, emeralds, sapphires, citrine, and diamonds were eye-candy for the tummy. After we made all of the flavors once, we needed to make another batch of our favorites, cinnamon and wintergreen. Can you guess why?

We loved to make, eat, and give away Mom's famous hard candy. When my girlfriends visited during Christmas vacation, each left with a jar of our tasty gems. We shared our multicolored treat with church friends and out-of-town relatives. One year we packed our candy into glass globes and stuck on the top of each a Styrofoam ball that resembled Santa's head; Santa had a coat of many colors from Ohio.

Royal brittle, brandied fruit, and cut-out cookies were some of the other treats that Mom made each December. So, why do I remember the hard candy more fondly than these other treats? Because we made it together. She trusted me like an adult to arrive home on time and to follow her directions. We shared an experience that was much more than making candy. The love, trust, and fun in our relationship was much more important than whether we were able to form the candy into perfect triangles; what was perfect was that we had each other. Mom and I treasured our Christmas candy-making tradition until I went to high school.

I learned that life has rough edges like our final batches of hard candy, but if we learn to accept God's plan instead of following our own, our lives may go more smoothly.

**Hard Candy to Make Treasured Memories**

Ingredients:

3-3/4 cups white sugar

1-1/2 cups light corn syrup

1 cup water

1 tablespoon flavored extract: cinnamon, wintergreen, orange, lemon, clove, peppermint

½ teaspoon food coloring of your choice to match the flavor (optional)

¼ cup confectioner's sugar for dusting

Directions:

In a medium sturdy saucepan, stir together the white sugar, corn syrup, and water. Cook, stirring over medium heat until sugar dissolves. Then bring to a boil. Stop stirring. Insert a candy thermometer to register heat between 300 and 310 degrees F, or until a small amount of syrup dropped into cold water forms hard, brittle threads.

Remove from the heat. Work quickly to stir in the flavoring and the coloring. Pour onto an oiled, sided cookie sheet or griddle pan. Use kitchen scissors to cut into strips and then triangles, or let the mixture cool before breaking it into pieces.

If desired, dust the candy pieces with confectioner's sugar.

Store in an airtight container.

**Christmas Conversations:**

Think about the special treats that you prepared with others for Christmas or at another time of the year.

Who was involved in the baking or creating process?

If you always looked forward to it, how did you feel?

Did the process go smoothly? What happened?

Did the experience affect or strengthen your bond?

How long have some recipes been in your family?

**Advent Actions:**

Have a treat exchange with friends and family. Taste the goodies and share the stories with the recipes.

# CHRISTMAS CARDS

*M*om always advised, "Your card should represent you." This is why my family sent religious ones with our Hope that they would give Joy to the recipients. Preparing Christmas cards was quite a ritual when I was growing up in Dayton, Ohio. Our dining room table (which throughout the rest of the year my mom uncompromisingly kept clear) looked like an extension of the post office. Nativity cards were slanted in their original boxes with the envelopes behind them. It is still a mystery to me that we had three levels of cards in our giving process: top quality with some gold foil for our family and special friends, middle level with less glitz for church members, and smaller cards with embossed scenes for everyone else. Mom wrote with her fountain pen from Uncle Arden (which no one but she ever used) and dipped it into a bottle of Kelly green ink for her distinctive signature.

Can you guess who the solo worker was on the Hoop family assembly line? I got to lick each five-cent postage stamp and TB seal, in gratitude for my oldest uncle's recovery from tuberculous, before following Mom's instruction to "Make sure the stamps are on straight." Next, we bundled them with rubber bands, adding special notices provided by the U.S. Postal Service: "Out of Town Mail" or "Local Mail Only." Snail-mail was the only mail. Some years we sent more than a hundred cards.

Mom opened another USPS extension at the home of their December Sunday School party. All of the members brought cards for each other; my parents sorted the cards and delivered a stack to each. The church friends also brought a monetary donation for the local hunger center that they otherwise would have spent on postage.

Mom's generation consisted of avid letter writers. All of our family members lived out of town, and we corresponded with them throughout the year. We felt good in knowing how much Joy our cards brought to the recipients. From Mom I inherited the correspondent gene. I love to send personal paper communications because I can imagine the recipients' smiles; they know it's from me because I write only in green ink, as Mom did.

Selecting and sending a religious Christmas card contributes to my Advent mood; it helps me to visualize that night in Bethlehem. It seems to be getting harder to find religious cards, though. Often, I send a golden foil-lined picture of exotic camel-riding Magi because sometimes when I answer the cards that I receive, I include the message, "Wise Men Still Seek Him." My card leaves no doubt that my Christmas is Christ centered.

At that first Christmas, there were no Christmas cards, but people still got the Word out that the world had a new King. Centuries ago, the Shepherds could not have comprehended over a billion and a half pieces of mail sent in December. Similarly, we may not be able to grasp the ways technology will provide for us to get the Word out during this century. Cards or computers? Or, phone? Choose the best way for you to communicate the coming of Jesus.

**Christmas Conversations:**

Think about Christmas cards that you have sent and received.

What card can you give that represents you?

What causes you to feel Love when you send or receive Christmas cards?

How does the card you send reflect your feelings about Advent and Christmas? How does it "represent" you?

Have you saved special cards or notes? Why those? What about them was/is so special?

How do you think technology will influence Christmas correspondence? Has it already?

**Advent Action:**

Send a special snail-mail card to someone who you know would love to receive one.

# JOY

# EXPECTING JOY

*B*y the third Sunday in Advent, I was feeling the Joy of the upcoming birth of Christ when I lit the pink candle. Why is the Joy candle pink, different from the other three? Maybe because whereas we may not always feel Hope and Peace or have human Love, we will always know that Jesus brings Joy. The comfort of a dinner routine at my table, and taking time to observe the already-lit candles for Hope and Love, helped me to welcome Joy tonight.

I love Advent! It's all about the anticipation and preparation for the arrival of Jesus. Most women take this time of year as seriously as if they were actually expecting. Our family situations may change, but the one thing that will not is the amount of work that women assume they will need to accomplish before the due date of Christmas. Can we learn to take clues from the original mothers in this story, Elizabeth and Mary? They were overjoyed to be expectant mothers and not concerned with the details of how that happened. True, they had more-miraculous things to discuss than we do, but they took time to meet and support each other. They exemplified that all things are possible with God. They were joyful.

Some of us like the rush of this season, as if we are expecting a real baby. So, we set out to accomplish in twenty-four days what expectant moms do in nine months. We get in a tizzy to the point of exhaustion, similar to taking care of a newborn, but the baby has not even arrived. Relatives and friends like to pamper the expectant mother. During Advent, we should be doing the same for ourselves and others. Meeting and supporting each other, like Mary and Elizabeth did, could help us to find meaning rather than madness during Advent. The pleasure of preparing should be as much a focus as the expected result on December 25th. Are we so obsessed about the outcome that we fail to let spiritual growth be as vital as the desire for a healthy child? This Advent, let's add Joy to our desire to be ready.

Many pregnant women show a burst of energy in the ninth month that pushes them to "get everything done" before the baby arrives. It was a delight for me to prepare the nursery with gender-neutral pastel-green curtains, a crib with embroidered duck sheets, and a drawer of booties for tiny feet. Then, for some unknown reason, I was driven to scrub the bathroom floor and to clean the refrigerator. Our first-born son, Owen, changed our lives before delivery.

Advent is all about the anticipation and preparation by us for the arrival of Jesus and the Joy that He brings. Most of us had years when we could relate to Mary as an expectant mother, or we knew someone who could. I have fond memories of my "Mary years." I identify with the joyful meeting of Elizabeth and Mary; I felt similarly. During December, many women feel the same burst of energy as we prepare for Christmas. Thank goodness that as we work, we know the exact arrival date of the Baby Jesus; this baby changed everything.

Advent women are the planners, the decorators, the bakers, the shoppers, the wrappers, and the givers. We smile at the sign in the mall parking space, "For Expectant Mothers Only." We know that nearly every spot in the lot should have such a designated marker. It's Advent!

## Christmas Conversations:

Think about whether or not you feel a part of a community of women who are preparing for the birth of Jesus.

Can you relate to how Advent preparation is similar to preparing for birth or another new beginning?

Following the Joy-filled example of the meeting of Elizabeth and Mary, would you welcome a quiet meeting with friends and family specifically to talk about Hope, Love, and Joy?

Do you recall a burst of energy when you were expecting or someone you know who did?

## Advent Actions:

Record your Advent Joys on a calendar or in a journal.

If you are a morning person, answer this question to start your day. "Where can I expect to find Joy today?" Do you feel excited or concerned?

If you are a night person, answer this question. "Where did I experience Joy today?" How do you feel now?

Where did you see Christ today? Did you acknowledge Him in your heart, maybe even thank Him for showing His presence in your life?

# GLORIOUS GLITTER

When I was four years old I was given a miniature Nativity. I had no idea at the time that this gift was the start of my own crèche collection.

When we moved to Dayton, Ohio, my first Sunday School teacher was Mrs. Tweet. She was a grandmotherly woman who volunteered to teach energetic preschoolers about the people in the Bible. "Come in, come in," was her voice echoing through the stairway as we approached her classroom. She was there every Sunday. If you were not, she mailed you a postcard to tell you that she missed you.

On the last Sunday before Christmas, Mrs. Tweet handed out tiny boxes and said, "You can open them." Each of us held a miniature Nativity in our hands. As we raised them to eye level, we could peek inside the stable and identify the familiar figures. Mary, Joseph, and Jesus were molded from hard brown plastic with dainty dabs of paint to help us recognize them. The roof of the stable glistened with glitter. I loved it. This sprinkle of silver delighted me as a child and continues to spark this childhood memory.

Now, I have over fifty manger sets to display year round in a glass curio cabinet in the corner of my bedroom. Some of my favorites include the one inside the matchbox from Peru, a crocheted set from Nepal, the Holy Family carved from Israeli olive wood, and the polished soapstone figures from Zimbabwe. Each culture creates the scene with native materials and sees Him in its own way. My sparkly favorite has a place of honor on the top shelf.

An unexpected gift from my Sunday School teacher taught me to expect to find the gift of Christmas Love. Mrs. Tweet joyfully influenced my Jesus journey with glorious glitter.

**Christmas Conversations:**

Think about an adult who influenced your spiritual growth when you were a child.

Was that person a family member, or someone else?

Do you have any keepsakes from your childhood? What are they? Do they still mean as much to you as they did then?

"Train up a child in the way he should go: and when he is old, he will not depart from it" (Proverbs 22:6). Talk about what you have experienced related to this verse.

How can you help a child or an adult to find Joy during this Advent?

**Advent Actions:**

Tell a child about one of your favorite childhood memories and relate that he or she will also have memories to share.

Tell a child about the background of Jesus and His birth.

Give a crèche.

# CHRISTMAS SURPRISE

*I* hope that you have had the opportunity to participate in "Secret Santa," "Secret Pal," or a gift exchange by any other name at your workplace. During December, names are drawn by staff members, and participants plan and deliver surprises for one week. Unexpected treats can range from finding a cup of hot chocolate on your desk to hearing your favorite carol sung just beyond your office door. As an elementary-school librarian, I enjoyed the staff's Secret Santa experience as much as I did sharing in the child-like anticipation of Christmas with my students.

About twenty years ago, I was in charge of Secret Santas at Hopkins Elementary School in Mentor, Ohio, when I was on the social committee. I was disappointed when I drew the name of the secretary because I had ideas for a classroom teacher. So, I asked my good friend, Jane, to swap names with me. I was not suspicious when she politely refused to trade.

My Secret Santa was super to me. Treats included hand-crocheted snowflake ornaments and cut-out cookie Santas. One day my station wagon was totally cleared of the white stuff from yet another record-breaking snowfall. Later in the week, I opened the door to my Library Media Center and found it draped in miles of red-and-green paper chains. My Secret Santa even magically prepared a game for my sixth-grade lesson for *A Christmas Carol.* I was clueless as to the identity of my Secret Santa. It was obviously a creative staff member who was dedicated to doing whatever was necessary for me to have a joyful and memorable week.

Jane and I ate lunch together every day and shared ideas for lesson plans. She also demonstrated some newly learned crochet stitches. I could not believe that I did not recognize the obvious— until Jane revealed her identity at the Secret Santa party. I am still using the set of Santa mugs that she gave me that week. I should have guessed from the beginning that it was Jane because it was not like her to decline a request, but she could not reveal that she had *my* name.

It is possible that some coworkers have not been told about Jesus. The message of Christmas may be like their undisclosed Secret Santa. Let's not keep Jesus a secret. We should take advantage of an opportunity to have some fun with little gifts that can show them and us how to reveal the birth of Jesus as being the greatest gift. And, maybe we can give Joy more often during the year.

**Christmas Conversations:**

Think about December festivities in your workplace.

Have you sought out and connected with other Christians where you work? How do others respond to you as a Christian?

Do you wish "Merry Christmas" or "Happy Holidays" to others?

How does political correctness affect you?

**Advent Actions:**

Make a conscious effort to start or continue to develop a relationship with a coworker. See whether your efforts bring Joy to the other person and to yourself.

# Making Room

The Innkeeper was never mentioned in the Bible. We imagine an Innkeeper the night Jesus was born from these words in Luke, "because there was no place for them in the inn" (Luke 2:7). We envision Joseph desperately knocking and pleading for a room for Mary, who may have been in labor. We can't help but to judge the Innkeeper, whose beard was barely visible through the crack in the door. At least he offered Joseph and Mary a place that we know had a manger. Did the Innkeeper miss the entire joyful event?

How do we keep ourselves from missing the birth of Jesus? Not just at Christmas, but the rest of the year, too. How do we make room in our "inn"?

Like that inn in Bethlehem, my life as a retired, busy woman has been full: managing a house on my own, committing to church committees, and keeping friendships with friends. Until recently, if someone knocked on my door I opened it cautiously and took a peek, but it was easier for me to guard my heart rather than to open it.

Why was opening my door to make room so hard to do? Did I doubt that I would ever feel Joy again? Growing up, I developed relationships with neighbors, school friends, and church families. Remember how easy it was to unlatch your screen door? Perhaps that was because we could see who was there. Twenty-five years later, I continued the open-door policy while raising a family; relationships were readily available with the parents of my sons' friends from school, Boy Scouts, and church members. But now, most of these associations have moved on or away. Vacancy helped me to shut my door and keep it shut.

I had thrived on having Christian friends, especially with those team members on Volunteer In Mission trips. When Janet and I get together, we continue to be humbled as we accept that we met because of Jesus and extend this relationship to our friends in Liberia.

46

It was easier for me to make room for relationships across the ocean than to make room closer to home. I asked myself, "Why?"

Why did my door at home seem to have an automatic lock? Had I unconsciously installed an alarm system that reminded me not to add more to my life? Maybe it was because some relationships I had tried, failed; I could avoid more disappointments and possible rejection if I did not have relationships to lose. My insecurities were protected by the security-system sign near the front door. I was alarmed that new contacts would require time and energy. I had no interest in what else God had planned for me. Did others have this same feeling and this is why they appeared to have "no room"? I convinced myself that, like the inn in Bethlehem, my life was full; it was enough.

I had not participated in a Bible study group in over twenty years. One summer, my writer-friend, Sue, invited me to participate in the Gifts and Talents Survey with women on Thursday mornings. While taking this spiritual checkup, I loved the camaraderie and Joy I felt while spending time with new sisters in Christ. I had missed this kind of a connection and did not even know it. To my surprise, hospitality was a skill that was now prominent in my survey results. This inspired me to entertain at my new home; I made room for neighbors, hiking friends, and church groups.

Jesus was placed in a manger. He did not know that his parents were told "no room." Even a humble stable was a welcome place for the three of them. Mary, Joseph, Shepherds, and Wise Men made room for Him in their hearts, with Joy to the world as the inevitable result. This Advent, let's use our connection with Christ to make room for others.

## Christmas Conversations:

Think about your willingness to start new relationships.

If this is difficult for you, what are some things that keep you from opening your door?

What keeps your "inn" full?

It is important for each of us to make room for a new gift or an aspect of talent that is emerging in us or somewhere in our lives. What new thing are you making room for in your life?

Expect to experience Joy when we make room in ourselves to do more for others: to listen to others when they need a gentle and non-judgmental ear, to comfort people in other ways when they need us, and more. When we do more for others, we give Joy to them and to ourselves. Who are you today? Who will you be in several months? How are you becoming a person who is more open to yourself and to others? Christ in you is the fullness of you.

## Advent Actions:

Reach out to someone new or reconnect with an old friend for an "Advent Buddy" connection. Communicate with this person throughout the year so that you can continue to remind each other about "Making Room in Your Inn" for Jesus and His Joy. In that spirit, consider and share the following verse from a Christmas card that was given to me by a dear childhood friend who died a few years ago (I'm eternally grateful that she and I always made room for one another).

"No room for a guest
at the Bethlehem inn.
No vacancy—not even one.
May He not find
our hearts crowded, too.
May there always be room
for God's son."

# TREE TRIMMING

When I was five years old, we moved to Dayton, Ohio. After Thanksgiving our neighbors asked, "Aren't you going to have a tree?"

Mom answered, "Oh, yes. We always put up our tree on Christmas Eve."

The tradition to bring a tree into the house for Christmas was started by German preacher Martin Luther. One night when he saw stars through the tree branches, this reminded him of Jesus, who left the stars of Heaven to come to us at Christmas. So, he brought an evergreen tree inside for his children to share the Joy he felt.

We may have waited until the last minute to trim a tree, but not to buy one. The short-needled fir leaned against the house, propped in a bucket, as we waited for the big day. Bringing our tree inside was joyful for me, but not for my dad. On the day before Christmas, Dad impatiently sawed a fresh cut from the trunk. He complained as he struggled to shove the tree into our red metal tree stand with the green spidery legs. I timidly held the door open while the tree's bushiness put pressure on the screen door's spring. Dad tugged it into the living room. I could not understand why he was grumpy. Decorating our Christmas tree was something I looked forward to all year; I was excited and joyful. Why wasn't he? He acted this way only at tree-trimming time.

When I was older, Mom took me aside and quietly explained that Dad's childhood was dismal and the lack of happy Christmases haunted him. Thankfully, once the tree was inside, both the tree and Dad were centered. He even laughed when Mom commented that the first thing she decided about our new house was where to place the Christmas tree. Seeing him be happy made me feel much better.

Dad, Mom, and I decorated our tree. It was our family ritual. We always waited until Christmas Eve to trim our tree because all of our relatives lived out of town. With no extended family to visit, we created this Christmas tradition as our own.

The tree filled our small living room. Dad struggled to find enough space to stretch the strings of lights across the worn carpet to test the bulbs. We used large colored lights, now considered to be old-fashioned. We made sure that our Star of Bethlehem tree topper had a blue bulb. Mom was the manager as to whether or not we had too many lights on the top (always) or the bottom (never) of the tree. I could hardly wait to decorate.

Our ornaments were a family album. Mom told the story of our special ones as she unwrapped them. A faded rose and a fish from my great-grandmother, a silver Santa from my parents' first Christmas, and pink-and-blue hot-air balloons for the year I was born were the first on the tree. While we were hanging the decorations, Mom reminded me that during the winter the evergreen represented everlasting life. We spent hours hanging the solid balls, glass lanterns, and starbursts. Mom, the Tinsel Queen, patiently taught me to drape each strand individually to catch the sparkle from the ornaments.

Today, even the sound of a vacuum reminds me of Christmas Eve. As Dad swept, he shouted over the hum of the Hoover, "Smells like a pine forest." Now, tree trimming was complete. We were not too tired to admire and comment, "The best Christmas tree, ever."

Finally, we arranged a piece of burlap around the base of the tree. It was plain brown, representing the humble birth of Jesus in a stable. Dad and I placed the Nativity under the tree, not quite complete because each year we added a few more figures from Woolworth's. In contrast to the blue light on the top of the tree, a yellow bulb highlighted the outstretched arms of the Baby Jesus.

All the lights glimmered when we turned out the living room lamps. Mesmerized by the glowing tree and the spirit of Christmas, I had no idea that most churchgoing families like mine were in the church's sanctuary for the Christmas Eve service. Instead, the three of us, brimming with Joy, celebrated the birth of Jesus in our bungalow. Like a Shepherd who followed the Bethlehem Star, I was filled with loving wonder.

## Christmas Conversations:

Think about your Christmas tree-decorating experiences. If they were special, what made them so?

If this was a family event, who was there and what roles did they play?

How can you help others to move forward from hurtful Christmas memories?

Perhaps you are no longer planning to trim a tree because you have moved or downsized, will be out of town, or do not have the energy. How will you decorate instead of having a tree? How will/do you feel about changing your tradition of decorating for Christmas?

## Advent Action:

Perhaps your ornaments can help you to tell your family's history and to recall Christmas Joys. Retell or record stories about your special ornaments.

# FATHERS

*J*oseph was unique in history because he is the only father to have a son conceived by the Holy Spirit. Why did God choose Joseph to be the earthly Father of Jesus? Joseph proved that he was a "righteous man" (Matthew 1:19) and a loving father to Jesus. Joseph's noble qualities made him God's choice and much more than a foster father in the Christmas story (Matthew 2:13-23).

The lineage of Jesus foretold that Joseph would be his earthly father. Listed in the first eighteen verses in the first chapter of Matthew, the fourteen generations of Abraham to David conclude with "and Jacob, the father of Joseph, the husband of Mary" (Matthew 1:16). It was important to trace Joseph's genealogy back to Abraham to fulfill the prophecy.

Joseph and Mary were betrothed in a community that observed Jewish law. Traditionally, in a Hebrew wedding, the groom was the center of attention. While Mary was visiting Elizabeth, Joseph anticipated her return so that they could start their life together with his family. Unexpected news arrived with Mary.

When Joseph met Mary after the visit, he was shocked by her pregnant condition. Initially was he hurt? Was he in denial? Was he speechless when it appeared that Mary had been unfaithful? Upon seeing her condition, Joseph knew that Jewish culture expected him not only to divorce her but also to condemn her. Instead of acting upon the expected penalties for adultery, he offered love and mercy to Mary; he chose not to disgrace her and to secretly send her away. In so doing, Joseph revealed that he was a man of kindness with self-control. These honorable qualities made him God's choice to be the earthly father to the Messiah. While Joseph was struggling to understand this unbelievable situation, the Angel Gabriel told him in a dream, "Do not be afraid" and that he would take Mary as his wife for the baby was conceived by the Holy Spirit (Matthew 1:20). Joseph obeyed Gabriel's message and accepted Mary as his wife. By his faith, he believed he could be a good husband and father.

Joseph was a carpenter, and he taught Jesus to be one, too. With sawdust in his sandals, Jesus was proud to be known as the son of a carpenter and to learn more than wood- working skills from him. Joseph also made sure that his son knew Jewish law and followed religious traditions such as attending the Festival of Passover. Both parents took Jesus to the Temple when he was twelve, and they were amazed at what people were saying about Him. This is the last time that Joseph is mentioned in the Bible. Jesus entrusted Mother Mary to the disciple with whom he was the closest, John, son of Elizabeth (John 19:26-27). This plan leads us to assume that Joseph was not present for Jesus' public ministry.

It does not seem fair that Joseph often has a secondary role beside the Virgin Mary. He fulfilled the prophecy, protected Mary, and was a joyful role model for Jesus. Like Joseph, who did not need all the answers, we as followers of Christ will not always have them. We should learn to trust God, as Joseph did.

## Christmas Conversations:

Think about the Lord's Prayer (Matthew 6:10-14) and the role model that Joseph must have been as earthly father, teacher, and spiritual counselor for Jesus to begin "Our Father."

Do you think it is harder for people who do not have a loving role model for a father to trust God as a loving Father? If so, why?

When you pray, how do you address God? Do you use another name besides Father? If so, which name(s) do you use?

Have there been men in your life for you to follow? If so, name those men and reflect on your positive relationships with them. How have you been blessed by a fatherly person in your life?

Was there a time in your life when you were like Joseph and you did not have all the answers? If so, how did you keep moving forward?

## Advent Actions:

Write a thank-you letter to a fatherly person in your life or write directly to God, the Father.

# UNCONDITIONAL LOVE

*L*ove came down at Christmas. Because of God's love, the world will never be the same. When we celebrate Christmas we can receive this greatest gift of unconditional love. The perfect gift over two thousand years ago reminds us that a gift need not have to be unwrapped.

Unconditional love is different from the kinds of love that most of us experience. It is not like the feelings we associate with romantic love. Unconditional love is action. This love without conditions has no bounds and is unchanging, like the Love God has for us. Unfortunately, our daily lives tend to center around reacting to love rather than acting with a love action that expects nothing in return.

Over the years, I witnessed complete love by observing Dad taking care of Mom. Mom was diagnosed with arthritis, diabetes, fibromyalgia, and glaucoma. She had lost her sight and her mobility. Unconditional love is love without conditions, especially conditions that change when a couple ages together over fifty years. Every day Dad demonstrated tireless devotion and unconditional love to Mom. He prepared the correct foods, bathed and dressed her, and tried to make her happy in her isolation. He was her sole caregiver for years. His life revolved around her well-being, with no thoughts about himself. She affectionately called him her "chief cook and bottle washer." Such love clearly brought incalculable Joy and Peace to each of them.

Believe me, unconditional love was the furthest thing from my mind when I regularly drove the four hours to their home. On Fridays, I drove to southern Ohio after work to help them downsize the contents of their home. I was looking forward to less time on the road after they would move closer to me. By Advent the next year, with less time traveling, I thought, there would be more time for gift buying, wrapping, and mailing. But now, being a daughter was a priority; I am an only child. It was not easy to balance my other roles as a wife, mother, and career woman with the daughter role. I struggled with dividing my time and finding the right way to use my energy. I felt conflicted about the lack of support and unconditional love that I received in my own home, compared with what I witnessed between my parents.

Saturdays with them were exhausting. Sorting, organizing, donating, and gifting dominated our day. Dividing the paperweight collection among extended-family members, packing the myrtle wood pieces for my cousin in Maryland, and boxing vintage Fiesta Ware for son, Neil. (Mom was antiquing for Fiesta Ware when she learned that Neil had arrived.) Sorting the cookbooks and boxes of recipes from *Family Circle* magazine. Unlike Dad, I struggled with my patience while Mom handled each item and made decisions as she reviewed and relived her life. My body was tired from the physical work; my brain was drained from watching her make tearful choices. With so much more for us to do, Mom reminded me, "Tomorrow is another day."

Finally, it was time for bed. Dad flipped on the light in the spare bedroom and turned to me, saying, "Your bed has fresh pillowcases, and I turned down the sheets." Unconditional love in bedroom linens. His kind gesture overwhelmed me and I was choked up when I hugged him goodnight. Such a simple act of kindness made me feel more loved than I had felt in a long time. I treasured the unexpected return to being treated like a child by my dad. He had so much to do to care for my mom and to manage the house, but it was not too much trouble for him to do one more thing, for me.

The love between the parent and the child is the example most often used to define unconditional love. I am certain that my dad expressed this love without conditions many times when I was a child. But, it was important for me to recognize his gift to me as an adult.

I had dutifully come to help Mom and Dad because I loved them so much. Unexpectedly, I experienced the joyful rebirth of my spirit through Dad's simple, tender gesture. His action of unconditional love reminded me that I should be providing more of the same.

**Christmas Conversations:**

Think about unconditional love. Have you ever given or received it? If you received it, what were the circumstances? Which did you prefer— the giving, or the receiving?

"You can give without loving, but you can never love without giving" (author unknown).

What are your thoughts related to this quote?

Have you ever experienced an unexpected simple gift, one that you did not need to unwrap?

Have you given a gift that made you feel surprised by how much Joy it brought to the other person? What is the most-heartfelt example of unconditional love that you've ever experienced or witnessed?

Does someone in your family need a gift of unconditional love from you?

**Advent Actions:**

Give someone a gift that does not need to be wrapped.

Have a conversation about unconditional love with a family member.

# PEACE

# Light Shines in
# the Darkness

The fourth Sunday in Advent came for me to light the third and final purple candle on my wreath. As I lit the Peace candle, I thought of Jesus as the Prince of Peace (Isaiah 9:6). I was feeling less anxious and more peaceful as the darkest and shortest day of the year approached. Even with the four candles at different heights, they lit the room powerfully during my dinner.

A year earlier, I was feeling no Peace when I was newly divorced and my sons lived out of town. When December arrived, I had many things to consider now that I lived alone in a different house. Where would I place the tree? Would the wreath look okay on the door? I had already decided on easy and convenient "outside" house decorations: I ordered nineteen battery-operated candles off the Internet, synchronized them to turn on at 5:30 p.m., and placed them in the windows, indoors. When they automatically turned on the first time, I ran outside to see how they looked. Their flickering orange flames were surprisingly different.

I wanted those candles for my new house because I valued the memories of similar candles that I had left at our old house. Years earlier as a young family, decorating our first home in December had been special after moving from an apartment. We splurged on the popular electric single white candles, one for each window of our colonial. Because a house built sixty years ago had only two outlets per room, we also bought a lot of extension cords. Each of the twenty-four candles had a switch. When we turned them on for the first time that evening, we could not wait to see our house. We bundled up the boys and ran across the street, wide-eyed. I can still hear Owen's "Ahhhhh."

Our neighbors' windows had different candles; Jewish families displayed their menorahs as proudly as we did our candles. Each night for eight days they lit candles to celebrate the Jewish Festival of Lights, Hanukkah, which symbolized the triumph of light over darkness in an event that happened one hundred and sixty-five years before the birth of Jesus. Their holiday emphasizes that God makes miracles for those who stand up for truth and justice. A Star of David at a menorah's base reminds us of Joseph and Mary's lineage from the House of David.

On Christmas Eve, as we pulled out of our driveway toward our church, we admired the lights on our tree by the picture window and checked each window for candlelight. Our church's traditional candlelight service gave a peaceful glow from real candles, filling the sanctuary and our hearts. As we drove home, we were still in the moment of "Silent Night" that can be created only on Christmas Eve. Turning onto our street, we could see our house's shining windows two blocks ahead. The white lights on our tree combined with the glowing candles, leaving no question that this home was celebrating the birth of the Messiah. Our house was a beacon like the Star of Bethlehem.

On Christmas Eve we had a tradition: December 24th was the only night that we left our window candles on when we went to bed. They stayed lit throughout Christmas Day. This symbol of lasting light reminded our children and our neighborhood that this is "the night" our Saviour was born.

**Christmas Conversations:**

Think about how you have used lights for decorating. What is your favorite?

..."I am the light of the world. Whoever follows me will never walk in darkness but will have the light of life" (John 8:12). What difference(s) do you see/feel between believing in Jesus and following Him? Do you follow regularly?

"Peace I leave with you. My peace I give to you. I do not give to you as the world gives. Do not let your hearts be troubled, and do not let them be afraid" (John 14:27). How do you interpret this verse related to the Prince of Peace?

**Advent Actions:**

Use Google, Bible Gateway, or a similar online resource to locate verses about light. After you read them, select a favorite verse to post on your refrigerator as an Advent reminder.

Can you remember times in your life when God has been a light for you, or has either brought Peace to you or helped you to find it? If so, what happened in that event? Share your story with someone who will be open to receive it.

# BACK TO BETHLEHEM

*I* was crying while driving to southern Ohio. Because my parents had decided to move to an assisted-living facility, I knew this would be the last time for us to trim their Christmas tree together, and I was trying to make my Peace with such an inevitable situation. Several years earlier we had abandoned our tradition of decorating the tree on Christmas Eve, which had been hard enough to do. Whatever time was convenient for me to travel and assist them was the new date. Changing the day did not take away from the importance and Joy in this annual event. Advent is about coming, but also about going back through family history.

I knew that a helpful neighbor was planning to get the short-needled tree into the stand and into their ranch house. I dried my tears and pulled into the driveway, relieved to see the Christmas tree in position at the picture window. Dad had done his job; those huge old-fashioned primary-colored bulbs blazed "Welcome!" As I entered, Dad greeted me with a tired hug. I walked over to kiss Mom, seated in her lift-recliner. We both commented on the aluminum star on the tree's top, which nearly poked the ceiling. For decades, the blue light in the center of this star had directed us back to Bethlehem.

After lunch, it was time to trim the tree. Mom started her traditional role by handing each ornament to me. So many times she had unwrapped our family's history. Now, her arthritic hands were as wrinkled as the tissue paper. We listened as she retold the stories of our favorites: an ancient glass rose, the fuzzy teddy bear, and the Rudolph with the mink eyebrows. Mom and I knowingly chuckled at the difference between the ornaments for her grandsons. "Owen's First Christmas" had been cross-stitched by me on the satin ball for the first offspring. By contrast, Neil's, the second son, was a store-bought rocking horse; his name and date were printed on the bottom with a felt-tipped marker about two years later.

By the late afternoon my parents left for a doctor's appointment, which interrupted tree decorating. While stacking the empty ornament boxes, I moved the heaviest, unpacked carton marked "Manger 1964." I remembered how Dad and I had placed the figures under the tree. Maybe I could avoid a tearful, uncomfortable scene with my parents if I set up the Nativity while they were gone. I hoped they would be pleased and relieved to see that all was in order on their return. Instead, I was the one taken back when I lifted the flaps of the box for the last time in this house.

A familiar layer of ancient cotton padding protected the ceramic figures. As I removed wrinkly tissue paper that surrounded each piece, I recalled that we had gone to Woolworth's each December to purchase additional figurines until we had the entire set. Each had cost under two dollars, but it still took us years to buy every one. We had started with The Holy Family. Baby Jesus still had his arms reaching out to us. Layered beneath the cow and the donkey, the Shepherds were nestled next to the sheep. I stared at my favorite, Backward Sheep. The Kings came next with their royal gifts. The camels, the largest animals, were packed in the bottom of the box; we loved them so much that they even had a camel herder to attend them. For years this Nativity had meant Christmas to me. How would I feel about moving them to my house next Christmas?

Once the figurines were lined up on the carpet, I skirted the tree with brown burlap for the humble Baby Jesus. I lay on my belly and tied the golden-foiled star to the lowest branch; it wasn't easy, but I maneuvered a yellow light in front of the accordion pleats so that it reflected on the Christ Child. The Shepherds and their sheep semi-circled to the left. The Kings and their camels arrived from the right.

I leaned back to survey my work. All the Christmases of my life were present. As I knelt before the Christ Child, I started to cry; I sobbed, longing for those special Christmases that had been created for me by Mom and Dad.

The next year, my emotions were peaceful when I unwrapped the Holy Family and its memories in my own home.

**Christmas Conversations:**

Think about the hardest thing for people to accept about downsizing or possibly moving to a different location or their final home. What is it? How would you feel about it?

How does your new role make you feel?

How did those you assisted feel and behave with you as their caregiver?

"For everything there is a season, and a time for every matter under heaven" (Ecclesiastes 3:1). We have seasons in our lives, and Christ is with us as we move toward a peaceful acceptance of our lives. Does this verse bring comfort to you during transitions with loved ones? How does your new role impact your Christmas celebration? How can you continue to find Joy?

What are your longings for Christmas?

**Advent Actions:**

Decide the most-appropriate way to thank the people who have created new Christmas memories with you. Who are those people? What are those memories? How will you keep going forward with your new memory makers? How can you help each other to find Peace in difficult circumstances?

# OUTCASTS

*A* Shepherd tends, herds, feeds, and guards sheep. Shepherds are mentioned over two hundred times in the Bible; sixteen times in the New Testament. During Advent, we focus on the Shepherds who were awakened in their fields by Angels on the night Jesus was born.

A Shepherd's job was one that everyone needed but no one wanted to do. Not many chose to be outside twenty-four/seven, living with smelly sheep. Because Hebrews prized cleanliness, it was one of the most-despised occupations. At the time, a Shepherd had the same status as a tax collector; society looked down upon them as a group. Since they could not leave their sheep, they could not take a day of rest to honor the Sabbath; as a result, Shepherds had no social standing or voice in their community because they could not enter a court of law.

I would imagine that tending flocks in the fields is usually a rather peaceful occupation. So, the Shepherds must have been startled and terrified when the night sky blazed with light! Did the sheep sense their panic? Were the Shepherds comforted when the Angel told them not to be afraid? God chose this unlikely shunned band to be the first to hear about the birth of Jesus. They were not only lowly but also isolated. Whom would they tell? God's immediate plan was to spread Joy. The second chapter of Luke states, "... I bring you tidings of great joy, which shall be for all people" (Luke 2:10). God's intention was to bring gladness, and He continues his exaltation when he singles them out, "For unto **you** is born this day in the city of David a Saviour, which is Christ the Lord" (Luke 2:11).

God trusted these simple men to seek the Christ Child. The Shepherds quickly left their fields and entered Bethlehem, filled with wonder at the sight of Joseph, Mary, and Baby Jesus in the manger. When they told Mary about their joyful experience, she pondered this in her heart. Their news was a comfort to Mary and Joseph. Then the Shepherds returned to their flocks glorifying and praising God.

If God had not sent the Angels to the Shepherds first, they probably would have been the last to learn about the Saviour's birth. Instead, God sent the message to everyday people at the time, which again gave evidence to His Word in the Bible: "The last shall be first and the first shall be last" (Matthew 20:16). These Shepherds would never forget that night, nor will we.

God continues to send messages of Hope, Love, Joy, and Peace to everyday people. I, for one, will try harder to be open to recognizing and receiving it as humbly as the Shepherds did.

**Christmas Conversations:**

Think about those who are the "lowest" in society today.

Does this reminder of Jesus' humble origins increase your compassion for the "lowest"?

Does it encourage you to wonder whether another great person might come from similar circumstances to positively influence the world?

When have you felt lowly or the least? How has God comforted or been there for you? Or, if you did not sense His presence, who was there for you?

What can we do to make sure the message of Jesus' birth reaches "all people" today?

About what do you think God would send an angel to say, "Do not be afraid?"

What makes some feel fearful rather than Peaceful about hearing the message of Christianity?

**Advent Action:**

Write an Advent prayer that has you glorifying and praising God.

# Unfulfilled Expectations

Christmas stockings were always a highlight of Christmas morning for me because we opened them first. The number of stockings at your house is a timeline of your family. Hanging stockings is directly related to your family, which can reveal both positive growth and unforgettable loss. My personal stocking history: three, two, three, four, one.

Three stockings hung on the back of the front door when I was a child. My stocking was solid red. My name was straight-stitched in white yarn across the top. I was glad that it was stretchy and flexible. Legend has it that the first stockings were filled by Saint Nicholas for unwed daughters of a poor man; he left gold coins so that each would have a dowry to take into a marriage. Following this tradition, Mom wedged foil-covered chocolate coins into the toe of my stocking next to an orange; she insisted that I experience the citrus scent she had longed for during her Depression-era Christmases. In my parents' stockings, each tiny wrapped box could be seen through the netting. I will never forget: one year, in our stockings, each of us received a wristwatch. No matter what we received, we always shared Love and Joy.

Two stockings lay under our tree for my first married Christmas. I learned that my husband's family, instead of using the same stocking each year, bought a different pair of socks for that year's loot. The first year, I had crazy red-and-white striped ones large enough for a hockey player and was surprised to find the matching sock in the toe. Eventually, this idea was replaced when Jeri, my sister-in-law, cross-stitched an exquisite stocking with my name.

After Owen was born, three stockings became four very quickly for us as a family. Owen and Neil were born only nineteen months apart. Soon, each of us had hand-stitched stockings from Jeri. We displayed them like works of art on our mantel. She was happy that we actually filled them rather than just using them for decoration. I collected bargain items all year. So, during Advent I thought of myself not only as Mrs. Claus but also as the Stocking Stuffer Queen when I opened my stash and rediscovered puzzles, colored pencils, and gold coins to wrap. I always bought too much. Owen and Neil loved the overflow as much as what they found in their own stockings.

The four of us had such fancy stockings that I was inspired to make unique green felt ones for my parents. Because Dad was an upholsterer, his displayed tools of his trade: a pin cushion, cutting shears, and a yellow tape measure for the hanging loop. Mom's was decorated with things she loved: a Maryland map, cats, and books. The last year they were in their home, I filled their felt stockings; it was my turn to be Mrs. Claus. Although I was emotional to do for them what they had always done for me, I managed to feel Joy because we still had each other. But, it was not to be my most-bitter-sweet stocking memory.

Just two years later in October, my husband and I decided that we would end our marriage of thirty-three years; we agreed to a final Christmas with four stockings decorating our mantel. The boys were grown, but we still pretended that the stockings would be magically filled in the morning. After everyone went to bed, it was time for me to fill them. While standing in my kitchen on Christmas Eve, I filled my husband's stocking for the last time. As I blinked through blurry eyes, I felt for a bag of gold coins and lodged them into the toe of his sock. I sobbed and let the tears run down my cheeks. As I stepped into the living room, I was surprised that the glow of the Christmas tree made me feel peaceful. There, for the final time as Mrs. Claus, I hung stockings on our mantel. The stockings were filled to over-flowing, unlike my expectations for a happy marriage.

I cried when I wrote this essay. Honestly, it is still difficult for me to think about that final Christmas with the four of us. This tradition is too painful to continue. Maybe I need to accept that it is normal to have a part of my life where I have too much emotion to let it go. I do not hang One stocking; I will keep my mind open to the possibility that the number could change.

## Christmas Conversations:

Think about your family history by writing down the names of the people who have hung a stocking at your home.

Share your list with a family member. How do you feel?

In which year were you especially joyful to be adding one?

Is there a history of handmade stockings in your family?

Think about a year or years when it was difficult for you to hang stockings because of loss.

Life is filled with changes, and you have been through many. Changes during life can cause people to be more accepting of themselves and of others. How have your feelings changed about yourself? Jesus encourages each of us to Love and accept the whole person we have become. Consider doing this for yourself. Consider doing this for someone else, also.

Remember that Hope is the first theme of Advent. Try to embrace the person you are now and recall how faith in God was present in your life experiences. It is okay to feel sad or empty, to be longing and hopeful. Love yourself as Christ loves you.

## Advent Actions:

Write about one thing that bothers you the most about celebrating Christmas this year. Try to decide whether you hope this difficulty will be resolved or whether you can accept that for now it is always with you and a part of who you are.

# Where's the Baby?

*E*ach family of David's lineage did the right thing. The rush was over to be counted in the Bethlehem census; they made it to Bethlehem. Thousands of years ago no one was asking, "Where's the Baby?" on the night Jesus was born. Not until surprised Shepherds were startled by a star-lit sky and Angels announced the birth.

Just as Mary and Joseph were expected to be counted, Advent is the season of counting down to the coming of Christmas. Modern times have us focusing on the "to dos" more than on for whom we do it. My preparing for Christmas for our young sons was driven by how to replicate the seemingly perfect Christmases of my childhood. My young boys each had a Nativity set. Neil even had Joseph and Mary stopping at McDonald's. They knew not only that Santa was coming but also that Jesus was coming.

On Christmas Eve we were still watching football when the window candles needed to be lit. This was so long ago that the Cleveland Browns were in the playoffs. Attending the 5:00 church service was past possible, and we actually were considering skipping the 7:30 one.

Our two-year-old son, Neil, was still napping, and four-year-old Owen was content building with Lego blocks. In our hearts we wanted to do the "right thing" and go to church. Was it really worth the effort to get all of us out the door in thirty minutes? Were we going to allow football to keep us from experiencing what happens every year, but only once a year? It would have been easier to relax at home, look at the tree, and enjoy our traditional oyster stew now, rather than later.

Suddenly, we decided to break out of our TV-room huddle. With a tandem effort, we dressed the boys in their three-piece vested Christmas outfits with clip-on ties. An advertisement for Sears Photography comes to mind. My husband switched into a navy suit, and I felt festive zipping myself into a home-sewn poinsettia-print dress.

Lee Road was colorfully lit as we approached our Gothic-style church. A dusting of snow covered the lines in the parking lot, but we found a spot. We took the boys out of their car seats and rushed to the side door opened by the "Merry Christmas!" usher. Wedging our way past unfamiliar parents, we delivered Neil to the familiar nursery.

Then the three of us waited in line to enter through the arched door into the peaceful sanctuary. The first pews were as crowded as the inn in Bethlehem—not room for one more. The space holds hundreds of people and it was almost full. As we walked across the front of the sanctuary, we passed the setting for the tableau (the Nativity scene of the Holy Family). Purposely positioned spotlights focused on a wooden platform between the lectern and the pulpit. A small stool was waiting for Mary, and a primitive crib sparsely covered with straw was waiting for Jesus. My eyes teared when I realized that our last-minute choice to come to Bethlehem was the right one. As the organist started to play "Away in a Manger," we were grateful to those who made room for us as we squeezed into a front-row seat.

"Where's the Baby?" Owen loudly asked. Such an obvious question from a preschooler and one I needed to answer.

The young family costumed as Mary and Joseph silently walked to the stage holding this year's "Baby Jesus." The waiting was over. Owen was standing on the seat for a closer view as he pointed, "There's the Baby!"

## Christmas Conversations:

Think about a Christmas when your preparations included having young children.

How do past experiences influence what you think is the "right thing" to do for Christmas? What are those "right things"?

Can the "right" way to celebrate change? If so, how?

How can decisions about our human thoughts of uncertainty be resolved to feel Peace?

Were you ever part of the tableau (the Nativity group) on Christmas Eve? If so, how did you feel?

## Advent Actions:

Volunteer to offer childcare to a couple with young children so that they can prepare for Christmas.

Volunteer to hold babies in the church nursery during the Christmas Eve service.

# The Gift of Giving

*I* was in the seventh grade when I received the gift of giving. The local gift shop inside our grocery store was going out of business in July. A hand-written "Closing – Everything Must Go" sign announced that items would be reduced by an additional ten percent each week. The inventory of greeting cards, music boxes, and gorgeous glassware was dwindling faster than my days of summer vacation. Visiting weekly, Mom and I took advantage of the reduced prices and purchased Christmas gifts for our family. Mom knew name brands and was attracted to a tall vase. She tilted it with both hands and smiled knowingly when she read *Fenton Glass—American Glass Artistry* on its base. Swirls of blues and greens flowed over twenty inches from the bottom to the fluted top. Mom said, "It reminds me of Monet's *Water Lilies.*" Somehow, I was going to get this vase for her.

When Dad and I secretly visited the gift shop a week later, Mom's vase was still there. What a relief! Dad paid with cash and handed me the receipt. Now, I owed him $14.86. We sneaked the vase into the garage, where Dad did his upholstery work. He wrapped it in foam rubber and cotton padding and tossed it like a football into the rafters, where it was cushioned by rolls of tapestry remnants. It was easier to hide the vase than my emotions.

My stomach was gurgling and my face felt hot when Mom and I returned to the store. Would psychic Mom observe that I was not behaving normally? Empty card slots and barren white shelves greeted us. Mom bravely hid her disappointment when she realized that *her* vase had been sold. "Well, someone else will treasure it," she said thoughtfully.

School was starting and I continued to earn money to work down my tab. I cut the grass on our corner lot. Instead of pocketing the money, I subtracted the amount from the vase's bill. Dad also paid me fifty cents an hour to remove old covers from furniture. We often chuckled about our Christmas secret while he upholstered chairs and I made the cloth-covered buttons to match the new fabric. Finally, in October, I paid off the loan. It was easier to count down the money owed than the months to gift giving.

Right after Thanksgiving, I was getting as excited about Christmas as when I had believed in Santa. While Mom and I wrapped the out-of-town presents, she always said, "I never think about what I'm going to get for Christmas."

Don't ask me what I hoped for that year or what I received, because I don't remember. What I do remember is the anticipation of gift giving. I appreciated keeping a secret, earning a surprise, and visualizing Mom's expression when she would open the fabulous Fenton vase.

December lasted forever. Finally, it was time to unwrap Christmas. Mom struggled with the weight of the oblong box. She gently spread the protective tissue paper to expose the green-and-blue swirled glass and exclaimed, "Oh, my! You bought me that vase!" I still cherish her look of disbelief and delight. That was when I really understood the Joy of giving.

## Christmas Conversations:

Think about when you could not wait to give a gift, either at Christmas or for another reason. Recall how anticipation made you feel.

To whom did you give a special gift and savor the memory? Why, do you think, does such Joy ultimately bring Peace?

Is it hard for you to keep a secret?

"It is better to give than to receive." How old were you when you learned this?

Can a physical gift say something about the feelings you wish to express?

Do you have a special gift that you are giving this year? If so, what is it, and to whom will you give it?

Have you received a gift and felt the Joy of the giver? How did this feel?

## Advent Actions:

Take time to reflect on giving and on receiving.

Make a list of the most-memorable gifts that you have received and that you have given. Do you see a pattern? Has your focus changed? Which act, receiving or giving, do you prefer?

# CHRISTMAS

# CHRIST CANDLE

*I*t is Christmas Day and the waiting is over. Time to light the Christ candle. The white Christ candle is the tallest, surrounded by the other four candles of different heights. The Hope candle, the first, is now the shortest because I have been lighting it every night; its gentle glow has reminded me that celebrating Christmas will be different but Christ is the same. Christ delivers on the Hope that we can expect Love, Joy, and Peace through Him.

The white Christ Candle glows in the center of our Advent wreath and symbolizes Jesus as the heart of our lives.

During Advent, we have sharpened our awareness of the coming of Christ as we lit a candle each Sunday. Lighting the wreath reminded us that we are called to be followers of Jesus. We have revisited Israel's longing for the promised Messiah by going back to Bethlehem in our hearts. The messages of Hope, Love, Joy and Peace illuminated our lives while we anticipated the wonder of His birth and "rebirth" in our lives.

Our journey is complete once again. I loved the comfort of the familiar scriptures, the music, and the candle-lighting ritual. How was your Advent journey? Did your celebration sway unexpectedly like riding a donkey? Or was your journey just plain bumpy, like riding a camel? Was it as you expected? How we experience Christmas each year may change. What we thought was customary may never be possible again. Nothing was normal about the first Christmas in Bethlehem, but now we celebrate the events of that night. Change is hard, but with Christ as our constant, we can move forward. Perhaps we should never expect "normal" but instead learn to be faithful like Mary and Joseph. Because life often changes, we may want to use this book every year for Advent.

Our Advent wreath shines with five candles – the Christ candle plus one candle for each of the four Sundays in Advent. Its light helped us to rediscover comfort and Joy. Now what? Just as Joseph led Mary and Jesus out of Bethlehem, it is also time for us to leave. We do not have Joseph's directions in his dream or the visit from an Angel that told the Wise Men to return a different way. Will we follow their example and take a new path? Can you relate to "I am the way, and the truth, and the life" (John 14:6) in a different way? If we feel uncertain or even lost, do we know that we can recharge our faith in Hope, Love, Joy, and Peace? If we can refocus our feelings about uncertainty and anxiety, perhaps we will step forward to experience any or all of these themes daily with Jesus throughout the year.

The Christ Candle is arranged in the center of my Advent wreath in a star-shaped holder that I bought for this purpose. When it is time to put the Advent wreath back into the attic, I remove the candle from the glass star and place the white taper into a brass candle holder. I light it during the dark days of winter. The Christ candle continues to remind me that I am not alone. Just a few weeks ago, I rediscovered this when I got the courage to light the first candle for Hope. I am comforted to know that my Christian family will journey with me as we find Joy in the New Year.

One thing I learned this Christmas is that next year, I need to buy a bigger white candle. If I use a pillar rather than a taper for the Christ candle, I can symbolically experience the Joy of God's never-ending Love longer.

I like the idea that Christmas is always coming. We welcome Christmas Day on December 25th. The next day, Christmas is coming, again.

**Christmas Conversation:**

Think back to the Advent themes of Peace, Joy, Love, and Hope. Have you experienced a rebirth related to Peace, Joy, Love, and Hope?

When we light the Christ candle, we are reminded, "... What has come into being in him was life and the life was the light of all people. The light shines in the darkness and the darkness did not overcome it" (John 1:3-5).

The gift of Jesus was not just for people in one place, but for all people. Discuss your Hopes for the world and consider one concrete idea to bring light into darkness.

Did you have a conversation or an experience during Advent this year that you can share with someone who needs to receive comfort and Joy? What was it and for whom?

To which character in the Christmas Story did you most relate during Advent this year?

**Advent Action:**

Some of the suggestions in this book's Advent Actions require advance planning. Select one idea that you want to try for the season of Advent next year and begin to put your plan into action.

# THE EXALTED

We have allowed our creativity to assume more about our visitors "from the East" than what is actually reported in the Bible. Different Biblical translations refer to the Wise Men as Kings, Magi, or astrologers. Our word "magic" is derived from "magi." These travelers certainly added mystery to the Nativity Story. Twelve verses in Matthew (Matt 2:1–12) tell us all that is recorded about the Wise Men. When we review the facts in Scripture, we can see that this short reference has been long on imagination.

When the Wise Men arrived in Jerusalem they asked, "Where is the child who has been born King of the Jews?" (Matthew 2:2). This question was troubling news to King Herod, who feared a rival. As a result, Herod demanded his chief priests to tell him where the New King would be born. They answered, "In Bethlehem of Judea; for so it has been written by the prophet" (Matthew 2:5). Deceitful Herod sent the Wise Men to Bethlehem and told them to report to him so that he, too, could worship the baby.

The Wise Men fulfilled the promise in Psalms 72:11: "May all kings fall down before him." They continued to follow the Star in the East. When they found Jesus, they worshipped him with Joy. Actually, we do not know the amount of time between Jesus' birth and when they visited. Scripture says they brought gifts to Jesus in a house and Mary was there. We do know that they brought three gifts: gold, frankincense, and myrrh. Historically, these items had deep meaning. Gold was given only to a king. Frankincense was the incense burned for God. Finally, myrrh was a burial spice. We do not know how many Wise Men delivered them.

Christmas Eve services present a tableau, usually with a young family as Joseph, Mary, and Jesus. The Shepherds meet them with Joy. Although the Wise Men were not present on the night Jesus was born, most pageants include them. The Wise Men enter carrying the named gifts for Jesus as we sing "We Three Kings." By combining the Adoration of the Shepherds and the Adoration of the Magi in the same scene, the idea is reinforced that Jesus came for all. God has the Shepherds arrive from the low country and the Magi arrive from the high country. All roads lead to the baby in Bethlehem and to Hope, Love, Joy, and Peace.

The timing of the visit by the Kings leads some denominations to follow the tradition called Epiphany. On January 6th, the twelfth day after Christmas, Epiphany is observed as the "manifestation of Christ by the Magi." When the Wise Men worshiped Jesus, they had a revealing moment; their perception of a king changed, and King Jesus would rule in a new way.

Will we be as wise as the Magi? Like them, can we stay on this different path now that we have followed the Star to Bethlehem?

## Christmas Conversations:

Think about how you would describe someone as wise or rich as the Wise Men.

What gifts do you have to give?

Did you have a sudden insight or understanding during Advent? An Epiphany?

Will you follow another way after Advent?

In the liturgical calendar, Epiphany lasts from January 6th until Ash Wednesday. In your daily life, what can you do to keep Christmas in your heart?

Consider how the rest of the world views us (Americans). Do you think they see us as kings? If not, how do you suppose they do view us?

## Advent Action:

Consider one gift that you have to give and how to offer your services to an individual, a group, or an organization.

CPSIA information can be obtained
at www.ICGtesting.com
Printed in the USA
LVHW051319121220
673922LV00008BA/817